Historic Walks in the Ribble Valley

by
John Dixon

Dalesman Books
1987

The Dalesman Publishing Company Ltd.,
Clapham, via Lancaster, LA2 8EB

First published 1987
© John Dixon, 1987

ISBN: 0 85206 899 9

Printed by Fretwell & Cox Ltd.
Healey Works, Goulbourne Street, Keighley, West Yorkshire

Contents

Cover illustration by Barbara Yates

Maps and line drawings in the text by the author

Whalley Parish Church (see page 14)

Shireburn Almshouses Stydd 1728. AD.84.

Shireburn Almshouses, Stydd (see page 47)

Introduction

WITHIN the boundaries of the Ribble Valley borough is to be found some of the finest country-side in the North West. The area is bordered to the north-west by the Forest of Bowland, an outstanding plateau of rolling hills and heathery moors, quartered by deep valleys. To the south-east Pendle rises leonine, her hind quarters resting in Whalley; her tail stretching over to Mellor. Between these great formations snakes the River Ribble, on whose banks are to be found some of the great halls and mansions of noble Lancashire families. The river enters above Paythorne and winds its way leisurely through its many curves, to leave this pleasant arcadia at Balderstone. As a result of boundary changes the borough now has sole ownership of that one unspoiled river, the Hodder, where from its watershed below the Cross of Greet, it flows through some of the most spectacular scenery in the North of England finally to enter the Ribble below the grounds of Stonyhurst.

It is an often repeated remark, that those who live in a place are not, as a rule, the most conversant with its history. For the native and stranger alike the intention of this book is to set right that imbalance that exists between known fact and fiction. It is hoped that the book will popularise still more a locality possessing many charms and attractions to the visitor, who has neither time or inclination to wade through the scattered and, in some instances, bulky and expensive volumes from which this little work is partly compiled.

The many places of interest recorded here are intended to be visited on foot, walking being the finest form of exercise that anyone can undertake. By this means one makes a small contribution to the maintenance of many old, and in some cases neglected, pathways within the Ribble Valley. All the routes used are definitive public paths, and never have I received anything but courtesy and help from the many farmers and landowners on whose land the paths cross. The walks have all been tried and tested by a number of my friends — many thanks for their help and useful remarks.

Your comments on the work or even contributions will be most welcome.

Destruction, Slaughter, Rout and Forfeit

A circular walk from Whalley, via Dinckley and Old Langho — 7½ miles (5 hours).
Bus No. 232/3 to Whalley. (Ribble)
Map: O.S. 2½ inch sheet SD 63/73.

WHALLEY Parish Church and the Cistercian Abbey deserve a full day's visit in themselves, but this walk is for those wanting to delve a little deeper into the history of the near landscape of this most ancient place. Communities have existed hereabouts for more than 3,000 years — each one leaving their mark upon the landscape. On our journey we shall walk in the footfalls of Celt, Roman, Norman and Medieval peoples through a world hidden away from the many who pass through the district. We shall visit many interesting sites, some of which you will return to many times to enjoy and share with others the idyll of their surroundings.
Follow Church Lane into the Square and on to the Abbey.

Whalley Abbey
The parent house of Whalley was Stanlaw Abbey in Cheshire, founded in 1178 for the Cistercian order, by John, Constable of Chester, on the eve of his pilgrimage to the Holy Land. Stanlaw proved to be a poor choice, subject to encroaches by the sea leading to a weakening of the foundations. In 1278, the great tower of the church collapsed, and two years later both fire and flood all but destroyed the edifice. In 1289 they obtained permission from the Pope to remove to Whalley with licence to build.

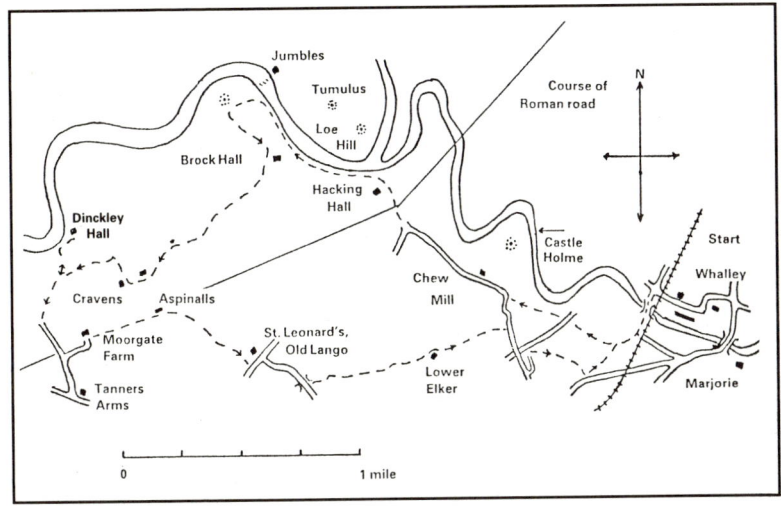

The first consecration was in 1306, and the church was begun in 1330. Licence to crenellate the building was given in 1339, and the first mass was said in the church in 1380. The Abbey prospered, and from all accounts the monks lived a merry life. The merriment was to come to an abrupt end in 1537.

In 1534, Henry VIII proceeded, with the consent of his Parliament, to substitute the royal supremacy over the Church of England for that of the Pope. This led to the rebellion known as the 'Pilgrimage of Grace', organised and led by the greater northern monasteries. John Paslew, Abbot of Whalley, was implicated in the rising; for this he was arrested and sent to Lancaster to be tried for high treason. Paslew was found to be guilty and was duly executed, his body being brought back to Whalley to be gibbeted on a site now known as Paslew's Mound.

After the Dissolution the Abbey was acquired by Richard Assheton of Downham and was adapted to make an Elizabethan manor house — a date of 1588 appears on a buttress. In 1923 the Church of England acquired possession and it is now the Diocesan conference and retreat house for Blackburn.

The drawing shows the north-west outer gateway. Built in the early 14th century, the passage is rib-vaulted in eight bays with a roofless chapel above. This was the main gateway into the Abbey along the ancient road that crosses Chew Mill ford from Blackburn and the west. To the north-west of the gateway runs an ancient

7

earthwork that may have been originally part of the early Celtic monastery of Paegnálaech that stood here in the 7th century.

The Abbey grounds are open to the public from 10am till dusk, with a small admission charge. The cellarium with the lay brothers dormitory, complete with both its lower and upper floors, can be found in the grounds of the Roman Catholic church to the west of the ruins. The chapel of Peter of Chester, early 12th century, is on the east side of the conference house.

Whalley to Chew Mill
Continue through the West Gateway to the railway arches. Turn left and follow railed-off pathway to Sunnyside Avenue kissing-gate. Pass through and walk on to go over stile. Follow path towards sub-station, over the stile and onward to the by-pass. Cross by-pass over stiles and follow overhead cable, via footbridge and stile, to Chew Mill.

Castle Holme, Chew Mill
Chew Mill, once a bobbin and clog-sole works, stands near to Bushburn Brook south-east of Potter Ford. This now by-road was once the main route from the west into Whalley, via Chew Mill ford. The Judge Walmesley Inn once stood at Chew — the licence was taken to its present site when the turn-pike was put through.

North-east from Chew, in a field by the Calder 'horseshoe', stands a square mound of around four foot in height. The mound is thought to be the site of a Romano-British temple, given its size and close proximity to a large Roman Veteran settlement across the river at Whalley. Roman coins have also been found near the mound. Others point to it being one of the twelve Anglo-Saxon castles built in Lancashire south of the Ribble during the reign of Edwin, king of Northumbria, 617–633, who was slain by Penda, king of Mercia, and Cadwallon at Hatfield Chase on the 14th October. At that time the River Ribble was the boundary between their two kingdoms. Castle Holme also stands near the crossroads of a major ancient trade route that goes back to the Middle Bronze Age (see below).

Chew Mill to Hacking Hall
Follow the road over Bushburn Bridge up the hill to a farm turn-off on the right. Walk down the left-hand farm track and pass through gate. Follow lane for 30 yards, turn off the lane as it bends to the left and cross the field keeping central of the two trees, over the 'moat' to a stile by the farm lane. Hacking Hall is on the left.

8

Hacking Hall

This fine symmetrical Jacobean mansion stands at the confluence of the Calder and the Ribble. Recently restored, it is a magnificent sight to behold when viewing from the riverside.

The house is dated 1607. and has on it the initials of Thomas Livesey, father of Sir Thomas Walmesley's mother. The Hall was rebuilt by Judge Walmesley of Dunkenhalgh, whose name lives on with a local inn — its sign bears the judges likeness. The principal room on the first floor of the east wing was formerly panelled in richly carved oak, one compartment of which bore the coat-of-arms of the judge. The carved oak was removed sometime before 1875 and taken to Dunkenhalgh. The moat of the original Hall can still be made out in the grounds of the building.

The great barn at Hacking is an old tithe-barn built by the monks from Whalley. Its massive cruck frame gives it a church-like appearance. The name Hacking, anciently Hakkying, is said to be from an old Anglo-Saxon community of hereabouts named the Haecingas. The meaning of the name is 'fish-wear'; standing so near to the confluence of the Calder, Ribble and Hodder, fish would indeed provide a good industry in such a spot.

Hacking Hall to Hacking Boat

Cross the farm lane and go over the stile into the next field, then on to the river. Loe Hill is the large mound to the right of the Boatman's Cottage. Behind the cottage you will notice an old barn, to the left of which is a tumulus mound (see Jumbles Rocks).

Hacking Boat

By the river a small pier-like structure can be made out — here stood the ferry known as Hacking Boat. Across the Ribble stands the boatman's cottage, sadly now falling into neglect. The boat can be seen today in Clitheroe Castle Museum in a fine setting. On a summer's day Hacking is a most pleasant spot to picnic and reflect on its ancient past.

Battle of Billington, A.D. 798

A mound on the opposite bank of the Ribble to Hacking, named Loe Hill, is thought by some to have been erected to commemorate the victory of Eardwulf, the Northumbrian King, in the battle of Billington. Some think the mound to be an ancient Bronze Age tumulus — others say it is only a mass of glacial deposit. Recent survey work on the mound has proved it to be man-made, but could not prove to what period it belonged. Finds from the battle have never come to light — what great store this land must hide!

Jumbles Rocks, Tumulus

The picture shows the old farmhouse of Jumbles, which still retains its original mullioned windows, standing on the opposite side of Jumbles Rocks. The rocks and the ford close by were well known to Bronze Age man, as four of their ancient 'roadways' meet here — the Hodder Valley up into Bowland, Rombalds Way up the Ribble Valley, the Calder Valley passing Worsthorne, and south-west over Mellor to Rivington. It is near this spot that we find traces of these early Celtic peoples. In 1836 Thomas Hubbersty, the farmer at Brockholes, was removing a large mound of earth in Brockhole Eases, about 500 yards from the bank of the Ribble. There he discovered a prehistoric burial chamber, formed of rude stones, containing some large human bones and the rusty remains of some spearheads of iron. On exposure to the air the whole crumbled to dust and were lost to study. Even given the 'iron' finds, archaeologists place the internment to the Bronze Age.

On the opposite bank of the Ribble, east of Jumbles next to an old barn, stands another tumulus. This was opened in August 1894. The finds were a young man's skull and a flint knife; a boy's skull; cremated remains of a body and a broken cinerary urn; and a child's skull. Remains of the funeral fire, being charred willow, were found in the centre. The find can be dated c.1250 B.C. The burial is one of an important person of that time, probably some local chieftain, buried near such a notable place as this crossing of roads.

Hacking Boat to Dinckley Hall

Follow the riverside path through the wood. On leaving the wood by a stile, follow fence to the left around the wood to Brockhall Farm lane. Go up the lane to the farmyard gate. Pass through the gate then through another gate directly on your right. Cross the bank of the field to go over a stile at the far end. Follow path alongside the playing fields (**do not go through the kissing gate**) *and greenhouses to go over a stile by the white gate. Follow hawthorn and privet-lined path on, over footbridge, up through the wood to go over a stile. Follow hawthorn-lined track past the barn and over the stile beyond. Cross the field on a left diagonal to Craven Fold farm lane. Keeping the farm to your right, pass the steel barn and cross the double five-bar gate. Turn left and go directly through gap in hawthorn hedge on the right. Cross the field heading for the gate and stile straight ahead. Cross stile and walk up to Craven wall-stile* (**do not go over the stile**). *Turn right and follow the hedge till you come to a gate and stile on your left. Once over the stile follow the left-hand hedge to go over footbridge and stile on your left (marked with sign 'Footpath'). Cross the field keeping the wood to your right and enter Dinckley Hall Lane by a gate and stile at the end of the wood. The lane leads down to Dinckley Hall.*

Dinckley Hall

Dinckley Hall stands by the Ribble next to the ancient Trows Ferry, so named because the early ferries resembled the shape of a trough. Remains of one of these early ferries were found further down the river at Salewheel and are now on display in Blackburn Museum. The last boat ferry was replaced by a footbridge in the early 1950s. The name Dinckley is of Celtic origin and means 'fort of the wood'; interestingly, the name of the neighbouring parish of Salesbury means 'willow, fortified place'. The two may refer to one and the same place and perhaps it was once a British fortified settlement of some note.

The Hall, a two-storey farmhouse, is much rebuilt and modernised from its original central hall and projecting wings. The north wing has disappeared, and most of the other parts have been rebuilt in brick. The east gable, however, retains its ancient timber crook construction, pointing to a date c.1500. The Hall's most notable occupant was John Talbot, who forfeited his estate for joining the King at Worcester in 1651 during the second Civil War.

In c.1610, a report on the clergy stated that at Dinckley there was a 'chapel but no reader'. Nothing is known of the chapel, though some place it to be the barn adjoining the Hall. A number of Roman altars have been found in the grounds of the Hall, one of which was in use as a cheese press — these were removed before 1725. Another Roman remain is built into the old stables of nearby Aspinalls Farm; rutted with wear it is one of a pair discovered here. The other, a conical-shaped edging stone, is now on display in Ribchester Museum. Aspinalls, and the road leading to it, stand directly on the course of the Roman road between Ribchester and Elslack.

Dinckley Hall to Old Langho
Return up the lane till you come to the turn-off to Moor Gate Farm. Follow the Roman road to Aspinalls. Pass Aspinalls and walk up to go through the far gate. Cross the field on a right diagonal towards a pair of oaks, then follow the track straight down to go over footbridge. Walk up the hill, bending round the group of trees, then aim for the gate on the left-hand side of the mock-Tudor Black Bull public house. St. Leonard's is off the road to the left.

Old St Leonard, Old Langho
The church of St. Leonard is said to have been built in 1557, with stone from the dismantled Whalley Abbey. Many of the stones are covered with ecclesiastical designs in the form of carvings. Inside the stoup (Holy Water font) and piscina (basin for washing the communion or mass vessels) may have come from the same source. The bench ends are carved with the initials of their owners with dates from 1688 to 1692. Ancient fragments of glass can be seen in the south-east window. In summer the chapel is hidden by a profusion of leafage and provides a welcome shade from the hot sun.

Old Langho is the original village centre, the other villages of

Langho and Billington only coming with the building of Whalley New Road. The earlier road ran from the New Inns, above Blackburn, along the top of Billington Moor then down to Whalley.

Elkar, at Billington, is the site of an ancient hamlet. On one of the old houses can be seen a carved corbel showing an angel holding a shield; this stone may also have come from Whalley Abbey.

The name Langho is a shortened version of the ancient spelling of Billington — Bil*langaho*h. Billington means either 'tun of the sword' or 'place of the Billinge', the Billings being a Brigantian tribe occupying the land between Whalley Nab and Hoghton Bottoms at the time of the Roman occupation.

Old Langho to Whalley Bridge

On leaving the church follow the road left to turn right at Keepers Cottage licensed restaurant, dated 1725. Carry on up the road past Hillock Farm Restaurant (notice the old stone showing a lion rampant and the initials of Thomas Hoghton) and over Skenning Bridge leaving the road by the first gate on the left after the bridge. Cross the field on a sharp right diagonal aiming towards Pendle to go over a stile. Cross the field to go over a stile in the far right-hand corner. Walk on over the footbridge and up to go over a stile in the fence. Then follow the track up to a lone oak and head straight on and over a stile near the farm. Follow the old farm track to Lower Elker Farm passing the barn on your right to find a stile near the farm gate. Cross and walk around the farm wall to the farm road.

Follow road down to Elker Lane. Turn right up the lane, over the by-pass, and leave the road to your left down old Elker Lane. At the bottom of the lane go over the stile on your right and on over the footbridge. Walk on heading for the far black gate, keeping the playing fields on your right. Go through the gate on your left and follow the hedge round to the farmyard. On leaving Whittams Farm follow the cinder road to the left down to Sunnyside Avenue kissing-gate. From here follow the road up under the arches to the main road. Turn left and walk down the road to Whalley Bridge. The Judge Walmesley is on your left, Terrace Row on the bottom right and The Marjorie by the river.

Terrace Row and Marjorie

Since being a young boy Terrace Row has always held a fascination for me. I used to imagine myself sitting on the balcony watching the skirmish between Roundhead and Cavalier on Whalley Bridge, such are a young boy's thoughts. The five early 19th century cottages, with their Gothic windows and access balcony, are a true delight to the eye.

The Marjorie, in the same Gothic style, stands on the bank of the River Calder just above Whalley Bridge. This charming home, with its castellated porch, was chosen as the cover design for British Telecom's 1984 Blackburn Area directory. Walk up the river and you will notice a large weir. The mill-race leading from it connects it to an old corn mill, which even today is complete with its old wooden water-wheel.

St. Mary and All Saints, Whalley

The parish church of St. Mary and All Saints is first mentioned in the Norman Survey of 1086, when a Norman clerk recorded of Whalley 'That the church held two carucates of land, and two oxgangs free of all dues'. Today the only certain Norman evidence is the south doorway with many-scalloped mouldings. The arch, however, is Early English. The Priest's Door is late 12th century and retains the original ironwork, and the bronze head of the knocker has the hair dressed in the style of the period. Inside the work is mostly Early English, and very grand. Pride of place belongs to the choir stalls which came from the Abbey, and the initials W.W. (William of Whalley, Abbot 1418–1434) give us a date. They are not in their original state, possibly a second tier of canopy-work existed. The misericords (shelfs on the underside of the hinged choir stall seats which, when turned up, supported the occupant during long periods of standing) are well preserved and are one of the most rewarding sets in the British Isles. A guidebook on sale in the church gives a full account of its many treasures.

In the churchyard stand three pre-Conquest stone crosses of the 10th century.

*   *   *

The rest of the day can now be spent in a leisurely exploration of the most ancient village of Whalley. Find the old corn mill and have a peep at the water wheel. Notice the old first-floor side window on the Whalley Arms; this came originally from Portfield Hall — it has the date 1781 and the initials R. C. The Old Grammar School, founded in 1547, is now an Adult Education Centre and the cricket field was the venue for the first ever Lancashire–Yorkshire Roses match. I could mention many more places of interest but I think I will let you discover those for yourselves. Have a good day and come again!

To Capture a King

*A circular walk from Low Moor Church, Clitheroe, via Wadding-
ton, Talbot Bridge and Bashall — 8 miles (4 hours).*
Ribble Bus No. 200 'Centrelink' from Clitheroe.
Map: O.S. 2¹/₂ inch sheet SD 64/77.

FOR the casual and regular visitor to Clitheroe this walk offers a
little taste of the district's surrounding charm and often hidden
delights. Waddington and Edisford Bridge are popular stopping
places for day trippers, yet concealed close by are enchanting
microcosms of rural life thankfully secreted and preserved from the
rude intrusion of maddening crowds. The walk takes in 14 sites of
mostly historical interest through delightful rustic settings.

Low Moor Church to Brungerley Bridge
*Cross the stile to the right of the garage and follow the path over four
more stiles into a field. Cross the field on a slight right-diagonal to go
over a stile. Then turn right and walk on to a field gate and stiles. Go
over the stile on the left of the field gate and follow the right-hand
hedge to corner stiles* (**do not go over stiles**); *here follow field hedge,
left, over the brow of the hill and down to go over a corner stile. Cross
the field on a right diagonal to the riverside path. Waddow Hall can be
viewed across the river. Follow path up-river to Brungerley Bridge.*

Brungerley Bridge
Brungerley Bridge is one of many bridges that before recent
boundary changes used to link Lancashire with Yorkshire — as a
stone set into the bridge tells us. In the days before the bridge was
erected people crossed the Ribble by way of hipping stones set into
the bed of the river. These were sited above the modern bridge.
These stones were fraught with danger, due to the narrow channel
between rocks forming a deep, slowly circulating whirlpool. Many
an unfortunate traveller has met their end whilst traversing the
swell. The legend of Peg o' Nell (see below) originated here. It was
she, it claims, who took the victim to the watery depths of the river.
  Local folklore tells us of an old inn that once stood near
Brungerley. The inn was known as 'Dule upo' Dun', from its sign

representing the Devil galloping madly along upon a dun horse. Legend holds that a poor tailor of the district sold his soul to Satan in return for riches. However, when finally the moment of his damnation came, the Devil repented and allowed the tailor one more final wish. The poor tailor seeing a dun horse standing close by wished that his greatest enemy should be carried of to Hell upon the steed's back. The Devil granted him his request, mounted the horse and rode furiously away, leaving the tailor to be thankful of his good wits that prevailed over his original greed.

Henry VI would remember Brungerley for quite different reasons. After the Battle of Hexham, the luckless Henry found his way to the Bowland District, seeking refuge first at Bolton-by-Bowland and later at Waddington. Whilst staying at Waddington Hall he was betrayed and later captured by John Talbot of Salesbury and others in 1464. They assaulted the Hall, but the deposed king escaped. A little later, whilst crossing the Ribble by way of Brungerley Hippings, he was overtaken and captured on the Lancashire side of the river, less than a mile north of Clitheroe Castle. He was thence carried bound to a horse to London and imprisoned in the tower.

Waddow Hall
Cross the bridge and follow the roadway to Waddow Hall entrance.

Waddow Hall

Look at Waddow Hall on the opposite side of the river — was ever a house situated on a site more beautiful than that? It is transcendently handsome, lying as it does at the foot of an eminence covered with trees which completely shelter it on three sides. To the front is a fine sloping lawn, at the bottom of which the Ribble dashes.

The house was originally built in Tudor times as a dower house for

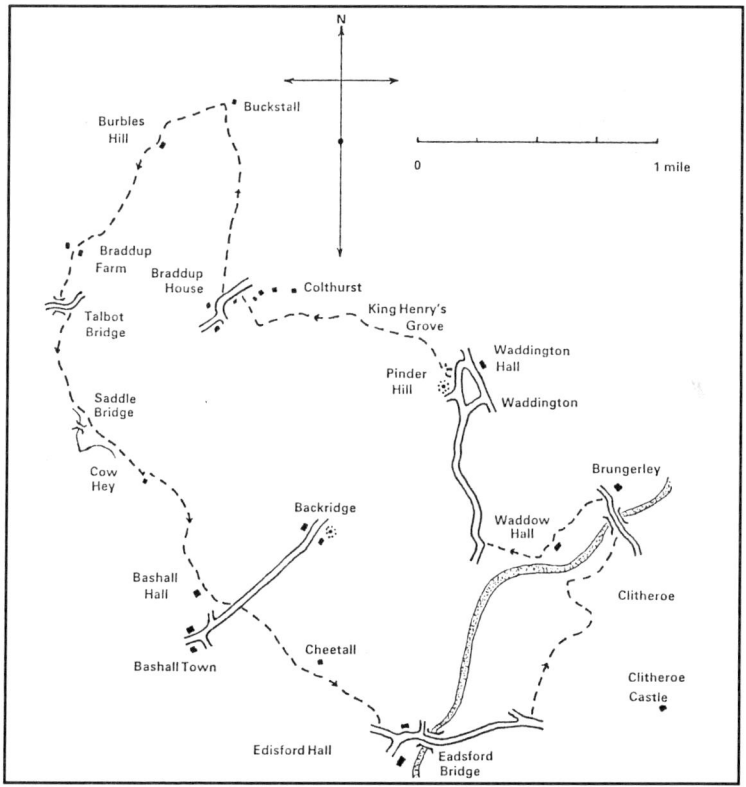

the Tempest family. In 1267, the name of Roger de Tempest of Bracewell occurs in the Assize Roll as Lord of Waddington. It was he who founded the parish of Waddington and paid a priest to hold service there. The lands remained in the Tempest Family until 1657, when the last of the male line, Richard Tempest, ruined the estate through his great extravagance. Richard cared more for the life of a dandy than that of a farmer, gambling and drinking his way through the family fortunes. This path led the foolish fellow to the Debtors' Prison on whose rat infested floors he was to meet the grim reaper.

The oldest part of the house is enclosed within the present building. This older building is shown on an oil paintng of 1690. Painted on a wooden card table it now hangs in the entrance hall below the main stairs. The Tudor house is now completely hidden behind the Jacobean hall. But the oak-beamed rooms, still in use as bedrooms, date back to the earlier building.

17

In the grounds of the Hall is a spring known as Peg o' Nell's Well. By the side of the well there is a headless statue said by some to be a likeness of Peg. Tradition has it that Peg was a serving maid at Waddow who fell in love with the eldest son of the family, greatly offending her mistress who expressed a wish that Peg would fall and break her neck. In reply Peg stated that if she did succumb to such a fate she would place a curse upon Waddow — every seventh year the Ribble would claim a life, though not necessarily a human life. One day Peg slipped on the ice around the well and the melediction was fulfilled. When 'Peg's Night', the last night of the seventh year, came round, unless an animal was drowned, some human was certain to fall victim of the curse.

The figure by the well holds in one hand a sceptre and in the other a book. It is similar to a statue of St. Margaret of Scotland. Peg is short for Margaret, and Nell is short for Helen — patron saint of the parish church of Waddington. Perhaps between the two is held the mystery of the statue's identity.

The Girl Guide Association purchased Waddow Hall Estate in 1928, and it is now used as a Commonwealth Training Centre.

Waddow Hall to Lower Buck, Waddington
Follow private road to cattle-grid near rear of Hall. Here follow footpath around the Hall grounds to go over double stile onto a trackway. Follow trackway to the road. Turn right and follow the road to the Lower Buck.

Waddington Hall
The Hall was restored by John Waddington in 1901. The present building is obscured from the road by high walls and tall trees, but a path runs by the side of the Hall giving a view to the rear. The greater part of the pre-Reformation building is still in existence. The original walls and windows can still be seen in the Great Hall, and the Monk's Room is also of the same early period. In fact the Monk's Room may be even older — some say that it dates back to the 11th century. The reason for the name is obscure, although it has been suggested that it arose because the room was used by monks travelling between the abbeys of Sawley and Whalley. Others tell of the Black Monk of Abingdon who is said to have betrayed Henry VI to the Talbot's of Bashall Hall.

Behind the panelling in the Great Hall is the entrance to the 'secret staircase' leading to a spacious room above known as the 'King's Room'. A modern carved cupboard shows pictures of

Henry's attempted escape — up the staircase to his bedchamber, down a ladder to the ground, and across the fields to Brungerley where he was captured on the Clitheroe side of the river. The poor fellow's name still lives on in the district — a King Henry's Grove is marked on the Ordnance Survey map.

Until a few years ago there was a small cave in Brungerley Park. Named King Henry's Cave, this may have been the site of a hermit's shelter (the changing course of the river has now obliterated all traces of the cave). A Hermit's Chapel of St. Oswald was known to exist in the Waddington district around 1444. It was common in those days for hermits to assist travellers across rivers, and the cave would have provided the hermit with some shelter. As to the site of the old chapel nothing is known. It may have stood by the old well in the grounds of Waddow Hall. Could the 'female' statue standing by the well be that of St. Oswald?

The Buck Inn

The Buck Inn, dated 1760, is one of the few remaining examples of a true country inn. The landlord serves a good selection of fine beers and ales to be quoffed by an open fire and good talk can be had without the tinny interruptions of an over-amplified juke-box — as is the case with many public houses today. By a wall at the bottom of the inn's cobbled entrance stands a horse-mounting block, a reminder of an older way of travel. A little way down the road are two sign-posts, one at a low level for the modern motorist while the higher sign harks back to the days of horse travel.

To the west of the inn stands Pinder Hill, a mound of glacial debris left after the last great Ice Age. During the Bronze Age, Pinder Hill was used as a burial ground and when the hill was excavated in 1887 two urns and some bones were found. Bronze Age axes have been found at Up-Brook Farm, Waddington, and in the rear garden of Waddington Hall are two low burial mounds said to date from the 9th century. The Bronze Age finds from Pinder Hill are now on display in Clitheroe Castle Museum.

St Helen's Chuch, Waddington

A church dedication to St Helen can often point to a post-Roman British population. Hellen was the mother of Emperor Constantine, and was said to have been born in Britain. The dedication continued to be popular into the High Middle Ages. The parish church of Waddington was established by Roger Tempest in 1267, who also paid for a priest to run the parish. Of the early foundation nothing remains. The tower is the oldest part of the church being erected in 1501. The font is probably also of that time. The benches in the Browsholme Chapel are late Stuart, and well worth a look at, being the most distinctive in the church.

The reference to Wada, an Anglo-Saxon chieftain, both in the church and on the gateway of Waddington Hall, must be treated with a large dose of salt. The story owes much to John Waddington, restorer of the Old Hall, a great romantic and benefactor of the church. His story goes that after the Battle of Billington, 796, the defeated Wada settled here with the remains of his army. The settlement grew and was known as Wada's Tun. Mr. Waddington thought himself to be a descendant of that ancient chieftain, a whimsy one can allow him in view of his good works in the village. In truth the name Wadington is of Anglo-Saxon origin meaning 'town by the wooded hill'. This meaning will be disputed no doubt.

An excellent history and guide by Nora Mary Goodchild is available from the church — it covers all aspects of the building with further notes on places of interest around Waddington.

Waddington to Braddup House, Colthurst

Take the lane behind the Lower Buck to a gated bridge. Here turn right to go up a driveway, pass the house, over the brook and stile into a field. Follow right-hand fence to go over wall stile. Bear left across the field to corner of wire fence. Here, keeping the fence on your left, walk on to go over a field stile. Follow right-hand hedge to go over a stile into field below Hollins Farm. Cross the field to trees to go over a stile. Now turn right and follow the iron fence to a stone bridge. Cross and follow right-hand fence, over stile, following right-hand hedge to a gated trackway. Here turn left and go over footbridge by the trees. Cross the field, keeping the two trees on your left, to go through a gate by the stone wall. Follow lane down to go through a kissing-gate on the right. Walk up the field, with the farm on your right and the clump of trees on your left, over to a stile. Cross and follow path to the road via kissing-gate. Turn left, down the road to Braddup House on the bend of the road.

Braddup House

Braddup House is an old farmhouse of the Late Stuart period. The present building is much restored; notice the stairwell windows — was this an original innovation? The old doorway is original, dated 1669, with the initials R.E.W.

Facing Braddup House is the entrance to Whinny Lane, an old trackway between Backridge and Waddington Fell. The lane is mostly overgrown now, providing a natural habitat for many types of wildlife. Wood mice scurry around, hare look to and fro and pheasant seek refuge from the barbarian's gun.

Braddup House. REW 1869

Braddup House to Talbot Bridge

At the foot of Braddup House driveway notice a field gate on the right. Go through the gate, up the field and through the next gate. Follow path up to go through gate onto farm roadway. Pass through gate on the right, and at the corner of the wood turn left and follow the fence by the wood, up, under fence, through three field gates, to Buckstall farm track. Turn left and go through gate, then follow right-hand wall on, through three gates, to the ruin of Burbles Hill barn **(do not go over stile into wood)**. *Walk around the back of the barn to the corner field post on your left. Cross the field on a left-diagonal, towards Kemple End (east end of Longridge Fell), to the end of the far hedgerow, go under fence and over stile. Cross the field on the same left diagonal to go over stile. Follow right-hand fence to Braddup Farm. Pass through farmyard to front of house. Walk a few yards down the farm lane to a field gate on the right. Pass through and follow over-head cables to brook. Walk downstream to Talbot Bridge.*

Talbot Bridge

Talbot Bridge straddles an old track linking Bashall Hall with Browsholme Hall. The track can still be made out running alongside the field path above Cow Hey on through Rugglesmire and Clough Bottom to pass over the 16th century arch of Talbot Bridge and on to Browsholme. The farmhouse standing near the bridge was once the old Woolpack Inn. This gives a clue to the travellers' trade in those bygone days.

Talbot Bridge to Saddle Bridge

On coming out onto the road, turn left and walk up for 50 yards to leave by a stile on the right at the end of the wood. Follow the right-hand fence down to a field gate. Pass through and follow right-hand hedgerow down to go through a field gate. Follow rutted track to the left, following stream down, to go through field gate. Saddle Bridge is on your right.

Saddle Bridge

Upon finding Saddle Bridge the eyes are greeted by a veritable fairyland. What tales could people tell of the folk who have oft crossed this enchanting bridge! Nestling in an idyllic setting the bridge rises like a huge stone saddle over the water. It is said that kind fairies erected the bridge in a single night, having taken pity on an aged woodcutter who was being sorely tormented by a witch who lived near another crossing further upstream.

Saddle Bridge to Bashall Hall

Follow the stream down to an old hedge-lined track, then follow the fence running alongside on the right of the track down to Cow Hey. Pass through farmyard and follow farm track down to Bashall Hall.

Bashall Hall

Bashall Hall was built by the Talbot family and is an uncommonly curious and impressive house. Constructed over many periods, Early Georgian and Perpendicular stand side by side. The whole is surrounded by walled gardens and accessory buildings. One of these buildings, an Early Georgian summer house with large vases on top, brings a touch of Versailles to Bashall.

The drawing pictures the old barracks of the Talbot's retinue of troops. Much half-timbered work still remains, and on the other side a wooden gallery runs the length of the first floor. Looking up one almost expects to see a trooper polishing up his boots or putting a shine upon his breastplate, so good is the restoration work.

It was from this Hall that John Talbot of Salesbury, his cousin Thomas Talbot, son and heir to Sir Edmund Talbot of Bashall, and Sir James Harrington set out to effect the capture of King Henry VI, who was in hiding at Waddington Hall. In the tumult of the Wars of the Roses many local families were torn as to where their loyalties lay — should they support the deposed Henry VI or the new king, Edward IV? Feeling that the tide had turned in his favour, Henry and his army crossed the border from Scotland into England, but they were defeated at the Battle of Hedgeley Moor and Hexham. Fleeing for his life Henry rode south and sought refuge for some time at Bolton Hall in Bowland, home of Sir Ralph Pudsay. This poor man, subject to fits of madness, could not remain from the authorities' notice long, and soon circumstances forced him to leave Sir Ralph's home and flee to Waddington Hall, which at that time was occasional residence of Sir John Tempest of Bracewell. Sir John was married to a Talbot, and soon news of the arrival of the Lancastrian King came to the ears of Thomas Talbot of Bashall. The Talbots, eager to gain favour with King Edward, rode out in force and surrounded the Hall where the King was at dinner. Upon hearing that the house was beset, Henry contrived to escape, and fled towards the river, hoping to put that between himself and his enemies. His pursuers, however, were too many and too eager for him. He was captured, after crossing the hipping stones, in a wood close by. From here he was conducted to London in the most ignominious manner, with his legs fastened to the stirrups of the sorry nag on which he was mounted, and an insulting placard fixed to his shoulders. On July 9th, 1465, the Talbots were granted a reward for this service. Even today some see the Talbot's action as an act of treachery, but given those troubled times who is to say what was right or wrong?

Bashall Hall to Edisford Hall
From the bridge walk up the road to leave by the first field gate on the left. Walk up the hill to a stile to the left of the tall tree. Cross the Bashall Town to Backridge road and over the stile opposite. Walk down to go over next stile by a field gate. Walk on towards the farm, over ditch, to fence. Follow fence to the right to go over stile on the left. Walk up to the top of the field to go over a stile on the right. Turn left and walk on to go through farm road gate. Walk down the road then over the stile on the left. Follow tree-line down, over stile, to

follow left-hand fence to end of small wood. From here head for the right-hand corner of the field, where the wall ends, to cross a stile onto the roadway. Walk down to the junction. Edisford Hall is the farm on the right.

Backridge

In Whitaker's *History of Whalley* is a mention of an ancient battle-field at Backridge: "In a line betwixt Waddington and Bashall, but especially around Backridge, have been discovered many skeletons, which from the manner in which they lay, must indicate the place of some great engagement. Among the skeletons was found a broken celt, and some brass fibulae were discovered about the same time and place." In Whitaker's mind this was a battle between Romans and Celts.

Local tradition tells of the 'Battle of Bassas Brook', where King Arthur and his forces defeated the Saxons under Tarquin forcing them back over the Pennines to York. Others suppose it to be the site of the Battle of Brunanburh fought near a hill called Weondun, where there had been a pagan temple, in A.D. 937. At the hill fort of Brunanburh, Athelstan defeated a Norse-British confederacy led by Anlaf of Dublin and Constantine, King of the Scots. The site has never been identified, and it may well be sited within Blackburnshire. Whatever the case Backridge holds its secrets well.

Edisford Hall

On first appearance Edisford Hall appears to be just an ordinary farmhouse, but close examination of this modest homestead will reveal some of its rich history. Still to be made out in the stonework at the rear of the house are a number of shields bearing arms. In particular note the lion rampant and fret of Roger de Lacy.

The Hall stands on the site of the old leper hospital and chantry of St. Nicholas. At the time of the Crusades one Orme of Hammerton gave two acres of land in Cheatale, Clitheroe, "to God and St. Nicholas the house at Edisford and the leprous brethren there for the health of my soul" and the souls of his family. The affliction of those poor men is now thought to have been elephantitis and not that of leprosy.

Edisford Hall to Clitheroe

Take the road over Edisford Bridge and follow it into town.

Edisford Bridge

The bridge is a medieval stone structure; the original ribs can still be seen under the central arch. In the 1300s tolls were taken for pontage (a toll for carriage of goods across the bridge) from travellers on the Lancaster–Clitheroe medieval way. The bridge was also the site of a battle some 800 years ago.

In 1138 King David of Scotland led his army on a raid into England; he detached part of his army into Yorkshire under his nephew, William fitz Duncan. With great carnage they laid waste the monastery of Furness and the province of Craven with fire and sword. On the 10th June that year William was attacked by the forces of King Stephen at Edisford Bridge. William routed this force and much blood was spilt by his men, forever staining the fields of Edisford with the quarted bodies of the King's men. This raid also penetrated into Coupland where Calder Abbey was plundered and its inhabitants put to the sword.

Old charters tell us that William fitz Duncan had already acquired the district north of the Ribble at Edisford along with Skipton in Craven by his marriage to Alice, one of the co-heiresses of William Meschin, the brother of Rannulf Earl of Chester. This being the case it seems likely that he made the attack because he was being forcibly kept out of his inheritance. Or perhaps he had a private feud with his neighbours, Ilbert de Lacy, lord of the honor of Clitheroe, who also held lands in Craven.

The battlefield has now given way to more pleasant pursuits. An indoor swimming pool, pitch and putt course, children's playground, an excellent caravan and camping site and a miniature railway all provide a splendid amenity for visitors to the district. The riverside path down to Siddows offers exercise for the motorists' legs. The hotel across the river is the Edisford Bridge Hotel and provides bar snacks and evening suppers. The pub sign depicts the sturdy bridge, and the seats below permit the weary traveller to rest his legs.

*   *   *

I suggest now a visit to Clitheroe Castle and Museum to view the antiquities held there. Then a short walk up to the castle keep where fine vantage points can be had to view the surrounding countryside, especially the walk that you have just undertaken. The town itself has many good shops and on Tuesdays and Saturdays an open market is held and provides the focal point where town meets country. The adjacent auction mart with regular cattle, sheep and horse sales adds a further unusual point of interest to the attractive town centre area.

Clitheroe Castle and Museum

Around 1072, after the 1069 rebellion in the North, William the Conqueror added Amounderness and the land between the Mersey and the Ribble to lands already possessed by Roger de Poitou. These lands along with Furness, Lonsdale and Cartmel made up a 'buffer zone' against Scots invaders. Roger, as Lord of Lancaster, built the castle and created a number of military fiefs giving unity to an area later to be known as Lancashire. At Clitheroe he erected a motte and bailey fortification with a wooden keep on the summit of a limestone outcrop. The castle got its first taste of warfare in 1138 during an invasion by the Scots, when William fitz Duncan laid waste the country around Clitheroe and routed with great carnage the English force stationed there.

For a bried period during the Civil Wars, Prince Rupert held the fortification for the Royalists. In 1644 Rupert passed through Clitheroe on his way to Skipton Castle, leaving Colonel Daniel as governor of the castle; he in turn placed Captain Cuthbert Bradkirk of Wrea in charge, who repaired the gateway and stocked the keep with provisions. After Marston Moor he abandoned the castle. It was then occupied by the Parliament and in 1649 was in great part destroyed upon the orders of Major General Lambert. Since that time the castle has remained in ruin.

In Castle House can be found Clitheroe's new Museum. This building was the former home of the Steward to the Lord of the Manor of Clitheroe. Inside can be found a wealth of local interest — a clogger's shop and printer's workshop, the old Hacking Ferry, Bronze and Iron Age finds, Roman artifacts and a fascinating display of geological material pertaining to the internationally renowned geology trail recently opened at nearly Salthill. The Museum also contains an oral history section; events, peoples and places are recalled by those who remember them well.

The Castle Museum is open to the public Easter–October daily 14.00–16.30; Bank Holidays 11.00–16.30. Admission charge. Tel: Clitheroe (0200) 24635. The keep and grounds are open throughout the year, free admission.

Lost Domesday Manors on the Roman Way

A circular walk from Whitewell Hotel, via Dunsop Bridge and Newton — 11 miles (5 hours).
Bus service operated by Leedham's Garage, from Clitheroe railway station.
Map: O.S. 2½-inch sheet SD 64/74 and sheet SD 65/75.

THIS section of the Hodder Valley is often described as 'Little Switzerland' and by far the most spectacular view must be from Tunstall Ing looking up the valley to Slaidburn. The walk offers a forever changing picture of both rural and moorland beauty through homesteads that go back before the Norman Conquest. The valley is first mentioned in 934, when King Athelstan granted lands to the west of the rivers Dunsop and Hodder to Wulfstan, Archbishop of York. The walk takes in 11 major places of historical and architectural interest along with other places also worthy of comment. So let us set off now on a journey of real exploration around this enchanted valley.

Whitewell Manor and Chapel
The picture above shows the Chapel and Manor House, or Keeper's House, as it was once called, as it would have looked in the early 1800s.

A chapel was established here around 1400 by Walter Urswyck, Keeper of the Royal Forest of Bolland. Records tell us that in 1422 extensive repairs and alterations were made to the manor and chapel which received a new roof and good windows. After the Reformation the chapel was dedicated to St. Michael the Archangel and received revenue formerly given to a chapel of that name standing in the grounds of Clitheroe Castle. The Clitheroe chapel had been abandoned and finally demolished during the Reformation. A curate from Whalley would preach once a month at Whitewell; rights of marriage and burial were performed at Clitheroe Parish Church. The enlarged building we see today was built in 1818. The windows are a tall straight-headed two-light type, but the boilerhouse window is of c.1400, displaying perpendicular tracery and is from the original building. Inside one finds a Jacobean pulpit, and a fine tapestry on the south wall depicts Christ's descent from the cross, based on a picture by Reubens on view in Antwerp Cathedral.

Walter Urswyck's manor house is now called 'The Inn at Whitewell' and some of the c.1400 walls still remain. This house was the Swainmote Court House; the Swainmote and Woodmote Courts met here. The Forest tenants also came here to give accounts of their doings to the Master Forester and his Keepers. The forecourt of the present hotel was once the old market-place for the district. The Whitewell Hotel is one of the very few inns that can rightly be described as a true country hotel — the layout is friendly and informal. Not long ago the landlord's son found a carved-out large round stone in the River Hodder near to the hotel. Experts declare this to be a mortar dating from the Middle Bronze Age — it is now known as 'The Whitewell Stone'.

Whitewell Hotel to Burholme Farm

Follow the road from Whitewell to Burholme Bridge. Just before the bridge turn right and follow farm track to cattle grid, then along riverside path to go over a fence. Follow fence up and onto the track again. Enter Burholme farmyard.

Burholme Farm

To the casual eye Burholme is just one of many pleasant Hodder Valley farmsteads, but a closer inspection will reveal far, far more.

On entering the farmyard take note of the sandstone milking shed on the left. A stone high up on the right side bears the date 1619, with the initials T.S. (Thomas Swinlehurst). Below this is another curious stone with a faded inscription that reads as follows: 'I JANE LOVE FOR TRUE TO W** AND FAITHFULL I WILL BE'

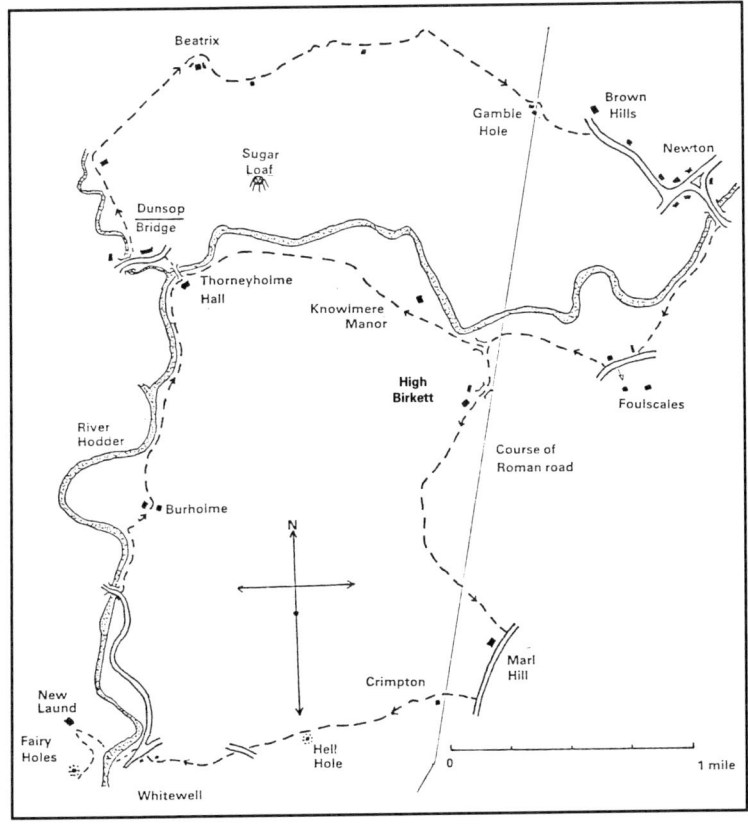

There was a Jane Walne baptised at Waddington in 1647, and a Janet Wilkinson of Burholme baptised in 1631. It is possible that the stone may refer to one or the other, but apart from its profession of love and fidelity, its significance is unknown.

Two other stones, known as 'Quaker Stones', are said to have been left by followers of the Pilgrim Fathers. They bear much faded inscriptions and dates of c.1735. Two further stones also bear inscriptions — one inside the building contains simply the letter 'W'; another, set in the bottom of a nearby stone wall, has inscribed the initials 'H.R.'.

To the right of the farmhouse doors stands a stone trough, carved out of a natural boulder; this appears to be of an age earlier than 1550. The higher barn is also of great interest. The timber of the cow stalls comes from old ships' timbers brought down through the

Trough of Bowland from Glasson Dock in the 18th century. Inside are some unusual corbles of the early 17th century, and used now as a doorstep is the base of a mullioned window of the same period. To the rear of the barn can be found an ancient stone washing and drinking well, fed from natural springs. This is from an earlier medieval period.

In the 14th century Burholme was far more than a single farmstead; it was then a small hamlet. It was here that the Woodmote Court was originally held before being moved to Whitewell in c.1400. A small chapel is also thought to have stood here at that time. This is born out to some extent by the fact that in St. Hubert's Church at Dunsop Bridge is an ancient stone font of around 1250. The font bears a brass plate indicating that it was found at Burholme. The font is one of two found; another now stands as a garden feature at Mill House, Dunsop Bridge.

On 10th September 1948, the late Father White of St. Hubert's carried out an archaeological excavation to try and locate the old chapel at Burholme. After several attempts, he came upon a line of stones, of large size and roughly shaped, revealing the foundations of a wall. This wall was calculated to face east. Later the outlines of other walls were traced, suggesting a building about 28ft. by 18ft. In the middle of the eastern wall there appeared the foundations of some projecting part, about 7ft. long by 1½ft. wide. A red tile floor of an ancient pattern, similar to some that are to be seen in Whalley Abbey, was found on this projection, also parts of others, which seemed to prove that whatever this old building was it had been given an expensive flooring. Last to be turned up were a door-socket in a heavy stone, and a rather massive stone carved simply by a skilled hand. By its shape and design it gave the impression of having served at the top of a pillar or arch as a beam support or corbel. Unfortunately, no more could be excavated.

The objects and walls revealed showed that there was an unusual type of building on this site in the Middle Ages. With the font at St. Huberts — found in the 1800s, and the likelihood that the projection from the eastern wall was an altar place, it all points to the site of the ancient chapel at Burholme first mentioned by T.D. Whitaker in his *History of Whalley* written in the early 1800s.

With permission of Mr. Chris Spence, the farmer at Burholme, and the Duchy of Lancaster Estate Office, a further dig was made by the Pendle Heritage Archaeological Group under the direction of Mr. David Taylor. This took place in September 1985 during a period of exceptionally good weather.

The site is situated on a spur of land alongside Fielding Clough to the east of the farm buildings. The excavation revealed an area of stone paving, made up of water-worn stones set on clay. The paving had been laid on an east-west axis, this being evident in the laying of the paviours and the direction of the joints. A fragment of the west wall was exposed, set near the platform on which the chapel had been built.

The place-name, Burholme, may be of a pre-Conquest date and mean 'the manor above the river'. Burholme is first recorded in 1343 as a vaccary (cow pasture); therefore a post-Conquest meaning would be 'water meadow with a cow-shed'. Burholme could well be the site of the now lost Domesday Manor of 'Bogewrde' — the first element being 'bow' (bend in a river as in Bowland/Bolland), the second being 'wearda' — Old Norse 'voroa', meaning beacon or cairn. The site of the beacon or cairn would be Kitcham Hill on Burholme Moor, possibly a Roman signal station given the fine views of the surrounding landscape and its close proximity to the Roman Road from Ribchester to Overbrough.

Silver and lead deposits have been found in Fielding Clough that runs through Burholme, and a crushing mill or other workings may lie nearby. Lead and silver have been mined in the Bowland area since Roman times.

Burholme Farm to Dunsop Bridge
Go through the farmyard, over footbridge and through gate. Cross the field heading for the far-off Brenand Valley, through gate and on through second gate to the river. Follow riverside path to Thorneyholme Hall. Walk down the driveway and turn left at the roadway to Dunsop Bridge.

Dunsop Bridge
We enter the village of Dunsop Bridge by way of the redwood-lined driveway of Thorneyholme Hall. Now an hotel, it was at one time owned by the Towneley family of Burnley. They gave the house to the Sisters of Notre Dame who used the building as a nunnery. The sisters also held Staple Oak, and at Dunsop they had a Dames School at Bridge End Cottages.

Dunsop is the gateway to the magnificent Trough of Bowland — that winding moorland track to Lancaster, and haunt of hardy hill walkers who wander over the vast Forest area. Just along the Trough road stands the Roman Catholic chapel at St. Hubert, patron saint of hunters. The chapel was built in 1864, and paid for by Richard Eastwood, estate agent to the Towneley family and a resident of Thorneyholme. The chapel consists of nave and chancel together, apse and bellcote. The west window and the apse have stained glass by Capronnier, dated 1865. There are numerous memorials in the chapel to the Towneley family. Notice the altar stone side pillars. They are decorated with four small carved horses' heads that represent Kettledrum, a horse that won much money for the Towneley stables and also won the Derby about 1862. In the picturesque grounds stands a huge white angel, a memorial to Richard Henry Towneley.

Dunsop Bridge to Beatrix
Before the bridge, turn right and follow tarmac track to Holme Head Cottages. Go over stile at the rear of the cottages and walk on for 50 yards to go over a fence stile on the right. Climb banking to go over wall stile. Walk up the field following the overhead cables on to Beatrix farm track. Follow track to the front of Beatrix Farm.

Beatrix (or Battrix)
The farmstead of Beatrix takes its name from an old Norse farming settlement of Batherarghes (Bothvar's Erg), a hill farm belonging to Bothvar (or Bathar), a Norse chieftain whose main settlement may have stood at Dunnow, formerly Battersby. Scandinavian names occur most frequently in the area north of the Ribble, especially in this north eastern part of the Whalley commote of the ancient Celtic realm of Blackburnshire.

During the 9th and 10th centuries the Norwegians held all the land that is now contained within the present boundaries of Lancashire and Cumbria; the Danes held central Yorkshire. The lands were colonised by Hiberno–Norse Vikings who came over from the Norwegian kingdom of Dublin. Their presence posed a great threat to the rule of the central and southern English kingdoms of Alfred, Edward the Elder and later Athelstan who finally succeeded in the submission of the North, culminating in the Battle of Brunanburh in 937, and the retreat of Anlaf's Viking army who fled to their ships moored on the River Wyre and returned to Dublin. The fact that certain place names have survived shows that the Norse influence and peoples lived on within the region.

In 1765, Beatrix was a hamlet of six holdings with three other holdings that lay on the edge of the old vaccary land. One of these has grown into the modern village of Dunsop Bridge. The other two holdings, Holme Head and Wood End, have changed little from their original size.

Beatrix to Gamble Hole Farm

Follow the track up and over the hill to 'Back of the Hill Barn'. Pass through yard and down to go through gate. On the same line walk down to the stream. Over the slab-bridge and follow the track up past 'Rough Syke Barn' to go over wall stile by top field gate. Follow track, through gate onto Bull Lane track. Walk on to where the track bends left and go through the small gate in the wall opposite. Walk across the field on a slight left diagonal to go through gate on the left of Gamble Hole Barn.

Gamble Hole Farm

A strange name — and again of Norse origin. Gamble comes from the Old Norse personal name of Gamel. The Hole? — well look to the right of the barn, and there you will see a large deep hole, the remains of an underground chamber whose roof has caved in. The whole area, especially in the field above Gamble Hole, is dotted with limestone shake holes. The Roman road between Ribchester and Overborrow cuts right through the farmyard and a section of the agger can be clearly seen crossing Pain Hill Moor above the farm. The farm and barn have a 17th century origin with some parts showing signs of an earlier date.

In 1731 Robert Parker was born at Gamblehole Farm and went on to study law at Lincolns Inn, London. In 1753 he was admitted an attorney of the Court of King's Bench. Late in 1753 he returned north to Halifax and joined a law partnership. By 1768 he was chief lawyer in Halifax. It was this Robert Parker from Gamblehole who was the main force behind the breaking of the 'Cragg Coiners' gang. The leader of the 'Cragg Coiners' was David Hartley — known as 'King David' — later hung at Tyburn, York in 1770, and buried at Heptonstall. Robert Thomas and Matthew, the 'hit men' of the gang, killed William Deighton, an excise man, near Halifax in 1769. Tried at York in 1770 they were discharged on the grounds of lack of evidence. But Parker collected new evidence, and as it was not possible to be tried twice for the same offence, he had them put up for highway robbery. Thomas was tried at York and was hung at Tyburn in 1774. Normington was arrested in the spring of 1775 and he too was executed at Tyburn.

Gamble Hole to Newton

Walk down the farm track and through the gate to follow right-hand track up to two gates. Pass through left-hand gate and cross the field on a left diagonal to go over stile in the far lefthand corner. Walk down the road to Newton.

Newton

Neutone, mentioned in the Norman Survey as part of the manor of Gretlintone (Grindleton), consisted then of four carucates of land. The ancient Town Field doles can still be made out in the field north-west of the village.

The village today has many fine 17th century houses, one with a Yorkshire lintel dated 1678 and the initials W.I.S. The Parkers Arms is a splendid Late Georgian building with a central Venetian window. Notice the ornamental cast-iron name plate with its Egyptian lettering. Newton Hall, across the way, is also worthy of note, and both buildings present a fine frontage to the village when entering by way of Newton Bridge from Waddington.

On entering the village from Gamble Hole, notice the Friends' Meeting House on the left. The house is a two-storey building with a date, 1767. The Quaker movement was started in Newton by William Dewsbury, an adherent of George Fox, in 1670. He faired less well in Slaidburn were villagers set upon him and drove him away. In Settle, Dewsbury was beaten unconscious by an angry mob and left to lie in the gutter. Picking himself up later, this man of strong conviction pursued his grand design only to spend 19 years in Warwick Gaol for his teachings and beliefs. On the main street stands John Brabbin's Old School House. It is a bland flat-fronted house with a date tablet over the door: J.M.B. 1757. Brabbin, in his will of 1768, left 20 guineas to endow a school to be held in this building 'for instructing all people called Quakers and six of the children of the poor not being Quakers.' John Bright, a leading light in the Quaker movement, spent two years as a boy in Newton and held many fond memories of the place, as is mentioned in his letters from later in life. The Congregational Chapel at Newton is the successor to a house known in 1691 as a 'meeting place for Protestant dissenters'.

Newton today is a quiet place were time seems to stand still; the Hodder flows leisurely by offering fine walks along its banks.

Newton to Foulscales

Once over Newton Bridge follow river path for 100 yards to go over stepped stile on your left in the corner of the wall. Follow riverside path, on over fence stile and on to riverbank trees. At the trees leave the river and walk up to go through gate. Walk up across the field on a left diagonal to go over fence stile. Walk on to go over stile onto the roadway. Turn right and walk on, over the bridge. Foulscales is on your left.

Foulscales

Here we find another old Norse name, meaning foal or fodder shed. A description will clarify this: here we have not one but two 'buildings'. Let us first look at the early 16th century work. The original building was a bastel type dwelling (the main living room occupies the first floor and is either patrician or defensive in origin) entered by steps up to the first floor. Notice the upper low mullioned windows and the medieval latrine set on corbles on the west end of the house. The ground floor would either house stock or fodder. The building appears to have undergone a change of usage some time during the 17th century, judging by the style of the ground floor mullioned windows. Seventeenth century conversion work can also be seen to have taken place on the barn opposite Gibbs Farm. Notice how the door lintels have been lowered and the doorways widened.

It is most gratifying to see such fine examles of vernacular architecture surviving, unspoilt and there for all to enjoy, giving us a fine picture of life in those times long ago.

The Foulscales Stone

This strange stone, 27in. x 11¾in. x 6in., was found in a field-wall near the road to Foulscales. Some antiquarians have declared that it bears early Christian emblems. Others explain that it is no more than 17th century graffiti or the work of an apprentice mason. I myself think that it may be an old vaccary or boundary marker; the 'T' might refer to a member of the Tempest family, landowners in these parts. A few years ago the stone was brought into the cellars of Knowlmere Manor for safe keeping. It has since disappeared from that safe spot; its whereabouts now is one of the local unsolved mysteries.

Foulscales to Higher Birkett via Knowlemere Manor

Walk back onto the road, turn left then turn right and walk down the 'Private Road' (only to cars) to a fork in the road. Knowlmere Manor is over on your right. Take the left-hand fork and follow track over the bridge and on up to Higher Birkett.

Knowlmere Manor

In 1258 the manor of Knowlmere was part of the holdings in Newton of Elias de Knoll. When his grandson, Rayner, who was Lord of Hellifield, died without issue, Rayner's younger brother Elias came into succession. He died leaving an only daughter Katherine; she married Adam de Hammerton and brought Hellifield Peel and Knowlmere to that family. When Sir Stephen Hammerton fortified his estates for his part in the Pilgrimage of Grace, Knowlmere was sold to Robert Parker in whose family it remained for many generations.

The Manor of Knowlmere was later granted by the Crown to Cuthbert Musgrave. It is now owned by the Peel family who purchased it from the Duke of Buccleugh. The Peels of Knowlmere are related to the Peels of Blackburn of Sir Robert Peel fame. Alice Peel of Knowlmere was a keen local historian and produced several good books on the Bowland area; one was a short illustrated history called *The Manor of Knowlmere* (Preston, 1913). Given her description of the Manor in the 16th century, the place was almost a small village in those days. The present house is built in the Gothic Revival style of late Victorian times; with its many gables and chimneys it presents an interesting picture. The parkland adjoining the Manor is exceptionally well maintained and pleasing to the eye.

Higher Birkett

Higher Birkett

Again more splendid examples of early farm buildings; notice the old studded door on an out-building at Lower Birkett — what great age must that be? Higher Birkett has a date of 1689, and many parts

36

of that date can still be seen on its centre front. The barn too is of that early period, very grand and solid looking.

As with Gamble Hole the Roman road passes here too, roughly on a line with the track approaching Birkett Bridge. Birkett Brook is worth following up onto the moor, past the old sheep fold and into the ravines to find waterfalls and deep crystal clear pools, all sheltered by a lush of overhanging foliage. An oasis within a wild moorland landscape and not to be missed.

The name Birkett means 'broad ridge' in the English and 'birch copse' in Old Norse. Given that it was first recorded by name in 1538, I would take the name to mean 'birchtree headland'. Whatever the origin of the placename both Higher and Lower Birkett are fine places to behold and well worth a visit.

Higher Birkett to Hell Hole
Pass through farmyard, through the gate and follow track to ford stream. Follow left-hand track up to the moor to go through gate in the top right-hand corner of the field. Walk downhill heading away from the wall to the stream. Cross the stream and follow up to find an old trackway on the left just before the ruined sheep fold. Follow track up the hillside to go over low broken wall. Head up to lone tree and wall. Over the fence and follow the wall on to the road. Walk along the road to leave to go up Crimpton farm track. Pass through the farmyard and follow left-hand wall/fence, past the tree-line onto the moor. On a slight left diagonal head for the pine wood, to go over stile set in the corner. Follow pine-lined avenue to go over stiles into field. Walk down to the right of Hell Hole Wood.

Hell Hole Pot
Hell Hole is a grade III listed cave, one of eight major limestone caves in the Bowland area. It has an open shaft situated within a small group of trees. Unless you are an experienced caver, and have permission from the Duchy of Lancaster Estate Office, Forton, near Preston, **do not** attempt to enter the cave. Also, **keep any children away from the edge** of the hole as a fall would be fatal. Ladders, ropes and other equipment are needed to attempt this cave.

Hell Hole to Whitewell
Walk on down to go over a stile by far left tree. Cross field and follow path to go through gate near small wood. Pass through gate on the opposite side of the road. Walk down to the far gateway. Pass through kissing-gate and walk down to Seed Hill Farm. Turn right

after the farm and walk down to gateway and onto the road above the
Whitewell Hotel.

*   *   *

The bus is not due until twenty past five so if time allows visit the
Fairy Holes; allow yourself a good hour and a quarter for the trip
remembering that this is the last return bus — it is a long walk back
to Clitheroe. On another visit may I suggest that you visit Tunstall
Ing, an old farmhouse above New Laund. As I have already stated,
the view from here looking up the Hodder Valley, is magnificent to
say the least. I hope to include this farmstead in a further book of
walks as it well deserves to be put on a regular trail.

Whitewell Hotel to Fairy Holes Caves
Walk past the chapel gate and farm buildings to enter the field via a
gate. Cross the field to go over a stile onto the river-bank. Ford the
river, crossing the gravel-bed in an upstream direction. Walk up and
enter New Laund farmyard by way of the gate; turnabout onto the
woodland track. **Do not follow track.** *To your right, on the bank, is a*
parallel path; find it, and follow it to its highest point. Here bear right
up the hillside on a slight left diagonal to find a limestone outcrop and
the caves.

Fairy Holes Caves
There are three cave entrances. The larger cave is 65 feet long, 6 feet
wide and 10 feet high; this leads to a blocked round chamber. In
1946 an excavation was carried out on the site under the leadership
of Reginald C. Musson. In front of this cave is a flat platform on
which were found occupational debris, including animal bones, a
pebble pounder used to extract marrow from bones, and sherds of a
Middle Bronze Age urn. The urn was collared with a design like
twisted cord. Two stone walls across the mouth of the cave were also
found, but no light could be thrown on their function. These
remains can be seen today on display in Clitheroe Castle Museum.

Opposite the Keeper's House at Whitewell is said to have once
stood a cairn of stones. When opened, in the early 1800s, the cairn
was found to contain a Kist Vaen (burial chamber) containing
remains of human bones. I have not yet determined a period as to
the date of this find. It may be connected with the 'Whitewell
Stone'.

New Laund Farm was a keeper's house in the Forest days, and the
inhabitants used the stepping stones, in the bed of the River
Hodder, to reach the Manor House at Whitewell. Today these
stones can hardly be made out and walkers must now cross the river,
heading upstream, across the gravel bed.

"Hark to Bounty"

A circular walk from Slaidburn, via Newton and Harrop Hall —
10 miles (5 hours).
Bus service operated by Leedham's Garage, from Clitheroe Railway
Station.
Map: O.S. 2¹/₂-inch sheet SD 65/75.

THE feeling I get whenever visiting this part of Bowland is one of stepping back to a time before the Industrial Revolution. Here there are no torn landscapes — only a great natural beauty that filled me with awe when, as a young boy, I first viewed this upper part of the Hodder Valley from the heights of Easington Fell. Even now after years of exploring the area that enchantment has never left me, throughout the seasons, and all they bring.

"Hark to Bounty", Slaidburn

Slaidburn was part of the manor of Grindleton in 1086, but in 1250 Grindleton was discarded by the de Lacy's as head of the manor in favour of Slaidburn. The Halmote or Chief Court of Bowland was held at Slaidburn (though occasionally in the old days at Waddington). The Court Room is still preserved and can be found above the Hark to Bounty Inn where its original furnishings of oak benches, a dock and witness box can still be seen — permission to view can be obtained from the innkeeper.

The name of the inn is a curious one and recalls an age when deer were hunted in these parts. The story goes that on a hunt day a visiting squire, the Reverend Henry Wigglesworth, was listening to the hounds giving voice outside; he heard that of his own favourite hound and his exclamation of delight gave name to the inn. Before 1875 it was simply known as the Dog Inn and was one of two inns in Slaidburn, the other being the Black Bull which since the 1930s has been used as a Youth Hostel enabling many generations to appreciate Bowland's magnificent countryside.

St. Andrew's Parish Church

The church is first mentioned in the 13th century — records from that time inform us that Hugh de la Val granted to the monks of

Kirkby Priory some interest in the 'Church at Slaydeburn'. The font is said to be of an earlier date, 1229, and once displayed Norman type decoration — due to re-working in the 1840s this can no longer be seen. The font cover is Elizabethan, similar to the one in Great Mitton church. The rood screen is a fine Jacobean piece with much openwork finery. The parclose screens are early 15th century work, with one-light divisions and a little thin panel tracery. The three-decker pulpit is an attractive piece of work from the Early Georgian period.

The exterior of the church displays its great age showing many periods of building — buttresses abound, most being of the 15th century. Near the tower stands a 14th century stone cross shaft with carvings on all four sides. It is thought that this once stood where the sundial stands now, atop the round stone steps to the west of the tower.

The church at Slaidburn was anciently known as the Wandenchapel, at that time being a chapelry dependent on Whalley church. The church stands on the edge of a field with the name — Bad Grove — possibly of Celtic origin. This area has a long history of occupation. In the last few years a Bronze Age mound was discovered in a field to the east of the church. A trial excavation in 1984 revealed what has been described as a 'trial lead palstave'.

Slaidburn to Ellerbeck Hall

Walk up the road to the Health Centre on the right. Follow footpath sign 'Wood House' through the wood, over the wall stile and follow river path to fence. Follow fence, around Tenter Hill, to the river to cross wall stile. Follow river path to go over another wall stile. Cross slab-bridge, then walk across field to the far wall, pass through gateway and follow right-hand wall round to Myttons Farm (dated 1846, T.W.). Pass through the farmyard and walk up the farm lane to go left as the wall on your left turns. Follow wall to go over wall stile. Follow right-hand wall, over the hill, over wall stile to follow right-hand hedge to go over another wall stile. Walk down the field heading for the right of the barn, then through the gates and onto the road. Walk down to Ellerbeck Hall.

Ellerbeck Hall

Ellerbeck Hall, also known as Wood House Hall, is a large 17th century building. The Yorkshire lintel above the front door is dated 1694, with the initials W.I.S. and I.S. — members of the Slinger family who lived here for many years. The house has many old stone mullioned windows but all the good stonework is covered in stucco.

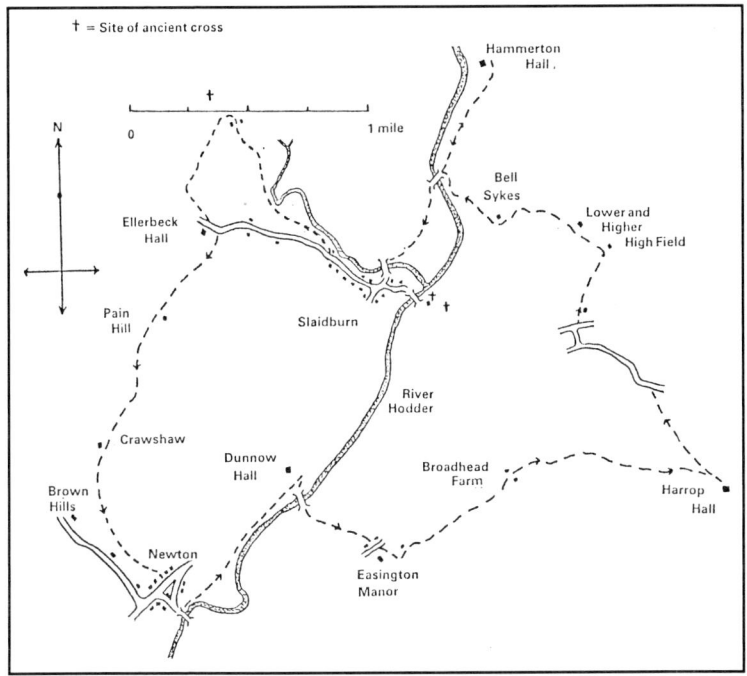

† = Site of ancient cross

In the 14th century the Abbot of Kirkstall held much land in the Bowland area. Woodhouse then was a stud for the Abbot's horses; the Cistercian grange was sited at Rushton on the upper Hodder.

Along Wood House Lane, at the entrance of Myttons Farm, is the stone pedestal of an ancient cross. Mossed-over and ivy grown, this stone once held the old pilgrim cross known as 'The Cross of Brown'. Crosses such as this were used to preach from, to transact business by and for public proclamations. The cross itself was probably damaged or removed during the Reformation or the Civil War.

Ellerbeck Hall to Newton

Walk on, over the bridge, then turn right and follow trackway to go through a gate. Follow path upstream along the brow of the hill to enter the field on the right by a gateway. Follow left-hand fence up, over fence, to go over wall stile. Keep following left-hand fence up to the right of Pain Hill Farm to go over corner wall stile. Turn right then left around the cow sheds and follow trackway on, through gate to the

41

end of the track. Walk to left-hand wall and follow up, past the wood, to go through gate, on into the farmyard. At the rear of the house go through gateway into the field. Walk down the field, keeping to the left of the windpump, to go over wall stile at 'T' in walls. Cross the field on a left diagonal to go over corner fence, ditch and fence into field. Keep on the same diagonal and walk up, over old trackway, to hedge. Follow hedge to go through gate on the right. Walk on, on the same line, to pass through far gate on top of the hill. Walk down to Newton.

Newton

Newton

The village of Newton is described in the previous walk. The drawing above shows Salisbury Hall, formerly Old Newton Hall. It was once the home of the Salisbury family who are mentioned as lawyers in Slaidburn in 1729. A walled-in square field near the river between Newton Bridge and Bargh Ford is still known as 'Salisbury' Flatts. The Salisburys left Newton in 1750 to live at Lancaster.

Newton to Dunnow

At Newton Bridge follow riverside footpath, cross footbridge, follow wall, over slab-bridge and wall stile. Left, following wall/fence to go through small gate on the left. Follow track on, through kissing gate to Dunnow trackway.

Dunnow Hall

Originally these lands were called Battersby until they were renamed Dunnow by Tempest Slinger of Catlow in Bowland. The Hall was built in the 1830s for one of the Wilkinson family, ancestor to the present squire of Slaidburn, John Norgrave King-Wilkinson.

Dunnow's first owner was to suffer a tragic loss leaving a dark cloud over the building. While honeymooning with his new bride in

Switzerland, the coach they were travelling in missed its footing on one of those wild Alpine tracks, sending it tumbling over the cliffside. Mr. Wilkinson survived the fall, but sadly his new bride was killed. From that time onwards none of the family could bring themselves to live at Dunnow Hall.

The old hamlet of Battersby that once stood here is mentioned in the Norman Survey of 1086 — Badresbi was then part of the manor of Grindleton and consisted of two carucates of land. The name Battersby means Byr or homestead of Bathar, a Norse Chief of these parts. Beatrix, a farmstead above Dunsop Bridge, was then the hill farm or shielding of Bathar.

Dunnow to Easington Manor

Walk along track to cross the river by bridge. Cross the field to go over footbridge and through kissing-gate. Cross field heading to the left of the far building on the left to go through kissing-gate. Follow fence round onto the road. Pass into farmyard opposite and walk through to Easington Manor.

Easington Manor

Esintune is another old settlement mentioned in the Domesday Book, although it never grew larger than two farmsteads. In 1284 the manor of Easington was held by Adam of Wannervill, one of the de Lacy tenants in the Honor of Pontifract. In 1324, when Bowland was in the hands of the Crown owing to the rebellion of Thomas of Lancaster, another Adam paid half a mark for respite of homage at the Bowland Court Baron. But he never resided at Easington.

In the 16th century the manor was held by the Banisters of Altham. The building, that has for the last ten years been subject to excavation by a local Pendle group of amateur archeologists, recognised now by a group of odd humps and bumps of earth, was built by Richard Bannister on the site of an old house of William Bannister, owner in 1552. In 1557 Laurence Bannister bought more of the same manor of Richard Tempest. The house was abandoned sometime around c.1700, when the family moved to 'Newhouse', a house they built above Slaidburn in the higher division of Easington. On demolition of the old manor house at Easington the original dated doorhead was built into the barn on Easington Lane. It has the initials R.B.A. – N.O.E. with the date 16**.

The dig on the 'bumps and mounds' has revealed the lower walls of the old manor house, being 4ft. 6ins. thick in places, along with the remains of the old fireplace. The excavation continues each summer and is attended by about twenty volunteers who work on the site daily, many of them camping throughout the holidays.

Easington Manor to Harrop Hall
Follow farm track down, past the barn, to go through iron gate on the left of the bridge. Follow stream up to enter field by the gate on the left. Follow streamside trackway to Broadhead Farm. Pass through gates onto the farm road. Turn right, then left following stream for half a mile to pass through gate. Follow stone wall on your left to go over footbridge. Walk up to go over wall stile. Walk down to stream and follow up, over wall stile, onto Harrop Hall farm road. Walk on to Harrop Hall.

Harrop Hall
Hidden from view between Witton Hills and Easington Fell can be found the ancient farmstead of Harrop Hall. The Hall is partly 17th and partly early 18th century. In the early 17th century the house was owned by the Moore family, who had moved to the area from Suffolk. The older low mullioned windows are from this period. Above the front door is a carved Yorkshire lintel with the initials R.L:L.L. with the date 1719. The initials and date appear again on a stone above the barn door. The Harrison family live here today and it is interesting to note that they use their barns, just as they were originally designed 250 years ago, with hay above and cattle below.

References to Harrop go back as far as 1274, when it was one of four wards in the Royal Forest of Bowland, these being Sclatbournewarde (Slaidburn), Baxsholfwarde (Bashall), Chepynwarde (Chipping) and Harropwarde (Harrop). Each of these wards was divided into vaccaries (large cattle farms), one of these being Harrop Hall. Harrop Fold was the site of the early hamlet. It lies on the east side of Harrop Fell and can be reached by a hill path which runs past Harrop Lodge and Lane Ends, down into the fold. The main approach to Harrop Fold is by way of one of the few gated roads that remain in the district.

Harrop Hall to Lower High Field
Walk back along the farm road to go through the gate on the bend. Walk up the field on a slight right diagonal, over the hill, to go over fence stile and on to the far trees. Cross the fence to the right of the trees onto the roadway. Walk up to the main Slaidburn road. Cross the road and walk up the track to the rear of the farm. Pass through gate on the right, walk on, over stile to follow right-hand hedge to Higher High Field. Follow lane down to Lower High Field.

Lower High Field cn.

Lower High Field and Bell Sykes

Lower High Field is a rebuilt 17th century house. A stone above the door lintel tells us that this work was carried out in 1876 for a person with the initials M.K.B. The lintel below is of a Yorkshire type. The decoration is intact but the initials are difficult to discern in full — W.W. and T.*.W. Other remains of the older house can be seen incorporated into the fabric of the barn — a two-light mullioned window and a doorway with a four-centred arched head in a splayed jamb. This type of door was usually secured by a draw-bar housed in a stone socket. It is good to see the re-use of older worked stone in any rebuilding process — it gives a place a solid and definite link with the past.

Bell Sykes is an attractive old farmstead and still looks much the same as when it was built in the 18th century. Notice the old cobbled yard, a feature common in and around Slaidburn. In the rear garden stands a handwound grindstone, its sharpening days long over.

Lower High Field to Hammerton Hall

Follow stream down to go through gate. Walk on to two large trees at the corner of the far stone wall. Follow wall down to Bell Sykes. Pass through the farmyard and follow track down to Holinhead Bridge. Turn right and follow track up to Hammerton Hall.

Hammerton Hall

Hammerton Hall is a splendid symmetrical Elizabethan mansion built on an E-plan layout, with three-storeyed wings. All the windows are mullioned except for the one in the first floor of the porch which has a transom as well. In the rear of the left wing is a stone spiral staircase, and between the hall and the wing the screens passage, with service doors, still survives. The present hall was built by Oliver Breres and it embodies the remains of the older house of the Hammertons, a powerful landowning family, owners of Hellified Peel and other large estates. Tradition holds that they could ride from Slaidburn to York on their own lands. Orme Hammerton, at the time of the Crusades, gave two acres of land and the house at Edisford 'to God and St. Nicholas and the leprous brethren there for the health of my soul'.

No Hammertons are now left in the district, due to the ill fated 'Pilgrimage of Grace' in 1536. It was through his share in that protest of the North against the dissolution of the lesser monasteries that Sir Stephen Hammerton was attained of high treason and executed at Tyburn. Being a knight he was spared the ignominy of drawing and quartering, and was hanged and beheaded. This harsh blow ruined the family fortune and killed the will to live in his son Henry, who died in 1537. He was followed in the next year by his young wife Joan, leaving two young daughters. What became of these girls and the two younger daughters of Sir Stephen is not known and remains a local mystery to this day.

Hammerton Hall to Slaidburn
Walk back to Holinhead Bridge, cross and walk up track to gate. **Do not go through gate.** *Follow wall to its end. Walk on a right diagonal to road bridge. Turn left into Slaidburn.*

*   *   *

The river bank at Slaidburn provides a good resting place while you wait for the bus to return. The icy cold waters of the Hodder will instill new life into tired feet. This river starts its life as a moorland stream below the Cross of Greet, flowing past Catlow Fell, soon to be lost like the old hamlet of Stocks in the vast expanse of the reservoir on the south-west of Gisburn Forest. The forest is extensively planted and almost lost inside this depth of pine are a number of 17th century farmsteads — Halsteads and Geldard Barn are fine examples. On leaving the reservoir the river, now chilled having spent time in the great depths, winds its way past Hammerton Hall to Slaidburn. Here the riverbank is a great attraction, providing a pleasant open space with cafe and car park. Onward the Hodder flows, past Newton and Knowlmere, to make a major southward turn at Dunsop Bridge. From here it flows past Whitewell to bend again at Stakes and meets the Loud at Doeford Bridge. Through many pleasant curves it flows through Chaigley and Bashall, under Cromwell's Bridge to enter the Ribble at Winkley Hall. As a result of boundary changes the Ribble Valley now has sole ownership of this unspoiled and sparkling river.

From the Crusades to the Civil War

A circular walk from the Ribchester Arms, Ribchester, via Stonyhurst College — 9 miles (5 hours).
Bus No. 11 to Ribchester Arms, Ribchester (Ribble).
Map: O.S. 2½-inch Sheet SD 63/73.

MOST visitors to the Ribble Valley take in Ribchester and Hurst Green, both attractive and full of interest in themselves. Yet between these two villages lie a number of ancient houses, preaching crosses and two chapels of great antiquity. This one walk will allow a far greater appreciation of the district than many visits without prior knowledge of the delights on offer to those a little more curious than most. The walk covers ten major places of historical and architectural note and others worth mentioning on the way, through some of the most beautiful and enchanting countryside in the Ribble Valley.

Ribchester Arms to Shireburn Almshouses
Walk away from the village centre, down the road to Stonebridge Restaurant, turn left down the lane and walk down to the Almshouses, sited on the left.

Shireburn Almshouses, Stydd
The Almshouses are uncommonly interesting, designed to catch the eye of all who pass down the narrow lane to Stydd. They were endowed by John Shireburn of Stonyhurst, in 1726, for five Roman Catholic widows or spinsters to live in, with coals and a small allowance.

Built in 1728, they are still maintained by the Roman Catholic church and were fully modernised in 1962. The three first floor bays have an arcade of rustic Tuscan columns with an open gallery reached by an open staircase, all very curious and engaging. In the front garden is an attractive well, alas no longer functional.

Shireburn Almshouses to Stydd Church
Walk on, over the bridge and up to the church.

47

St. Saviour Chapel, Stydd

The manor of Stydd was acquired by a preceptory of the Knights Hospitallers about 1265 from a more ancient hospital (the Hospitallers began in the 11th century as guardians of the pilgrim hospice of St. John of Jerusalem during the First Crusade, 1096–1144). Grants which have been preserved indicate that there had been an organised community at Stydd for at least fifty years previous; they refer to 'the hospital of St. Saviour under Longridge and to the master and brethren serving God there'. The Hospitaller's medieval chapel has seen much change to the original fabric over the years. The north side has two Norman windows and a small doorway with single-chamfered arch. The south doorway is an excellent example of Early English architecture, having clustered columns, with floriated capitals, supporting the deep moulded arch. The slit lancet south window is also of this period, but the east and west windows with interesecting and Y-tracery are of the late 13th century. The blocked doorway in the west wall may have connected the preceptory with a wooden balcony in the church. In the south wall are also two Perpendicular straight-headed windows.

On entering the sacred edifice the first object that strikes the eye is the Late Perpendicular font, which stands opposite to the south door. It is octagonal with eight carved shields bearing elementary motifs. Next we notice a late 17th century oak screen, of a very simple character, that separates the sanctuary from the nave. A simply panelled pulpit of the same period stands on the south side. In the churchyard stands a pedestal of an ancient cross, one of many to be found in the area.

A service is held in the chapel on the last Sunday of each month — a visit at such a time will be well rewarded.

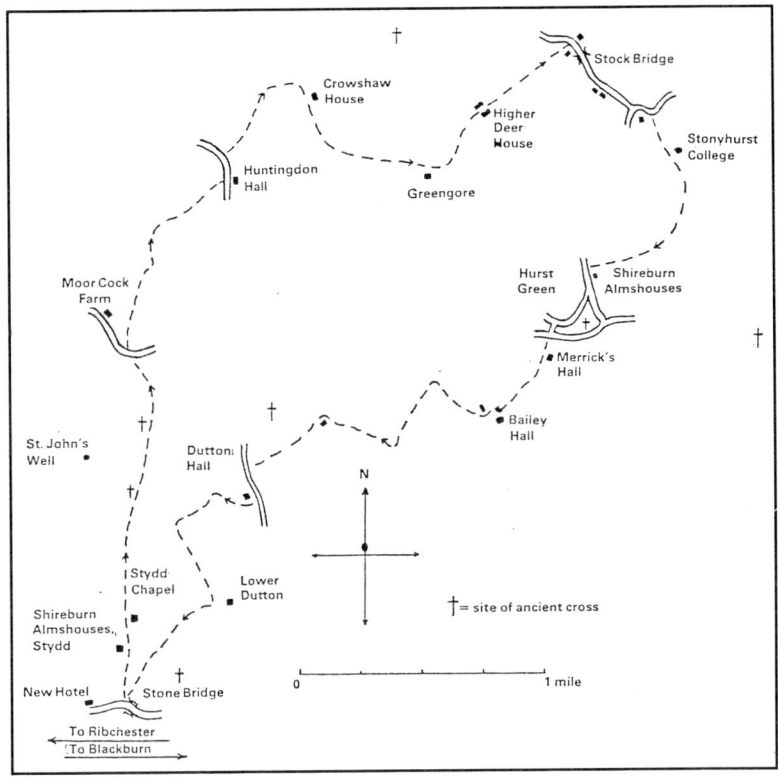

Map showing walking route with labelled locations including Stock Bridge, Crowshaw House, Higher Deer House, Stonyhurst College, Huntingdon Hall, Greengore, Moor Cock Farm, Hurst Green, Shireburn Almshouses, Merrick's Hall, Bailey Hall, St. John's Well, Dutton Hall, Stydd Chapel, Lower Dutton, Shireburn Almshouses Stydd, New Hotel, Stone Bridge.

† = site of ancient cross

N

0   1 mile

To Ribchester
To Blackburn

Stydd Church to Moor Cock Inn

Walk on through the farmyard, pass through two gates and over the stile by the red gate. Follow the well-worn track up the field to the right-hand corner gate. Over the stile and follow left-hand hedge to a footbridge (the remains of an ancient cross are in the corner of the field on your left). Cross the footbridge and walk straight across the field to go over a stile. Walk up the field on a slight right-diagonal to pass through a field gate. Follow track up to Duddel Hill Farm and on to the main road. The Moor Cock Inn is the first house on the right, up the road. The inn lost its licence in 1923; above the door is a strangely illustrated date-stone, 1775, with the initials B.B.

Moor Cock Inn to Huntingdon Hall

Walk back to Duddel Hill Farm entrance, on the bend of the road. Cross the hedge stile opposite. Walk on and through a gap in the fence by the tree line. Walk on up the field on a right diagonal to pass through a kissing-gate in the far right-hand corner. Left, over the bridge and after 20 yards turn right and follow the path up through the wood and over the stile. Follow left-hand fence, keeping to the right of the barn to a field gate and stile. Over the stile, and follow right-hand fence to brook stile. Over the stile, and follow the brook to the wood. Walk, right, around the wood and through the field gate. Follow the track around the brow of the hill, and on through an iron field-gate to Huntingdon Hall.

Huntingdon Hall
The Hall and lands in this part of Dutton are named after Robert of Huntingdon who came from the Abbey of Selby in 1277. After the death of his son, Roger, a feud ensued between Robert and Beatrix, widow of Roger, over the ownership of his son's land. Today all is peace and quiet with the Hall slightly hidden from view by tall trees. The Crombleholme family of Loud Mytham also have associations here. Richard Crombleholme held lands in Huntingdon and Bailey in 1588. The present Hall has stood on this site since 1619. It is H-shaped with a facade of mullioned windows, all in a timeless setting guaranteed to gratify both eye and mind.

Huntingdon Hall to Crowshaw House
Walk up the road to a gate and stile. Pass through and walk up the field on a right-diagonal to go over a fence stile. Walk down the hill, over a stile, to the right side of Intack Farm. Keeping the quarries on your left, follow the overhead power-lines to a farm track. Turn right and walk down to Crowshaw.

Crowshaw House
Crowshaw was part of the estate of the Clitheroes of Bailey. During the Civil Wars it was tenanted by Richard Holden, younger brother of John Holden of Chaigley, probably the recusant (one who held the Roman Catholic faith) of that name who had his lands sequestered by the Commonwealth of Oliver Cromwell.

This spot gains its notoriety from an incident that illustrates the turbulence of those times. A priest, discovered in the act of saying mass at Chapel House Farm in Chaigley, was summarily executed there. His severed head was flung over a fence where a Mrs. Holden of Crowshaw House redeemed it, gathering it up into her apron and smuggling it into her home. The head and other chapel trappings — missal, cloth, vestments and candles — were concealed and preserved as relics by the family. These were kept in great secrecy at Crowshaw until the establishment of the Jesuits at Stonyhurst when the relics could then be shown. In 1887 they were in the possession of the Holdens of Hill House, Woodplumpton, and an elaborate description was printed in the *Stonyhurst Magazine,* November 1887.

Crowshaw House to the Greengore
Walk down the farm track, pass through the field-gate and follow the rough old track to the Greengore.

Greengore
Sited on an old moorland trackway is the imposingly strange house of Greengore with its massive buttresses. Mention of the house was recorded in 1314, when 'Thomas de Greengore confirmed to Adam his son, certain land in Bailey, excepting the Greengore.' The name Greengore means 'Green Mud', and suggests that the land was partly marshy in bygone times. In the 15th century Greengore was used as a hunting lodge and is said to have played host to the Lancastrian Kings.

The huge buttresses point to the great age of the building and are obviously an addition, the windows being not earlier than Elizabethan. Notice the chimney-stack set on corbels — could this have been an old medieval latrine? Only an inspection of the first floor would resolve this point, but I personally doubt it. With its many stone mullioned windows the interior was well lighted for the period.

Greengore to Stonyhurst
Follow track down for 60 yards then cross the stile on your left. Turn right and cross another stile, then left, over the next stile into the wood. Follow path down, over the footbridge and up to go over a field stile. Walk on to Higher Deer House. Passing the front of the house, follow the farm lane to the roadway. Walk down the road, over Stock Bridge, past Stockbridge Cottages, on past the right fork, through the ornamental gate into the grounds of Stonyhurst.

Stonyhurst College
The most pominent house in the Ribble Valley is undoubtedly Stonyhurst. For centuries it was the residence of the lords of the manor until 1794, when it was placed at the disposal of the Jesuit Fathers of Liege. It is now one of the finest boarding schools for Roman Catholic boys in the country.

Many former pupils have gone on to achieve great note in their fields of work, perhaps the best-known being Sir Arthur Conan

Doyle, creator of Sherlock Holmes. It was Stonyhurst that gave him the idea and setting for his story *The Hounds of the Baskervilles'*. The artist William Turner, in his early days as a jobbing artist, drew Stonyhurst for an engraving — my drawing is taken from that engraving.

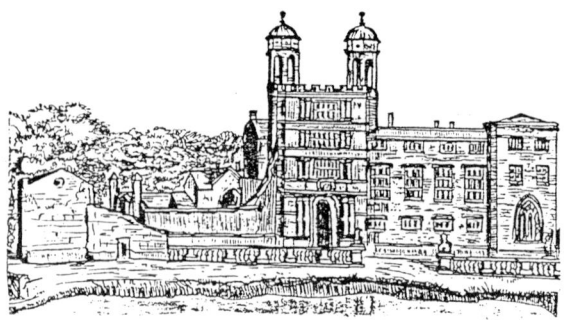

The building as we know it today was started by Hugh Shireburn around 1523, the major part being that of Sir Richard Shireburn who began work with the gatehouse in 1592. Additions and alterations, especially in the gardens, were made by Sir Nicholas Shireburn, who inherited in 1690, and started to live at Stonyhurst in 1695. He lost his only son in 1702, and died in 1717. His daughter, the Duchess of Norfolk, made a few further alterations. Then followed neglect and a change of ownership, and in 1794 Thomas Weld offered the house to the Jesuits of Liege. The Fathers had been driven from Liege by the horrors of war and the proscriptions of the French Revolution. They were induced, in consequence of the mitigation of penal laws against Catholics, to seek an asylum in their native country. The Jesuits added later buildings from 1799. The tremendous Church of St. Peter was finished in 1835, built as a proud response to the Act of Catholic Emancipation in 1829.

Stonyhurst contains many priceless treasures, the oldest being a 7th century copy of St. John's Gospel which belonged to St. Cuthbert, a relic from his tomb in Durham Cathedral opened in 1827. The binding of the Gospel book is the finest example of English leatherwork to survive from the Anglo-Saxon period. And strangely enough Stonyhurst overlooks Mellor Hill, one of the few places where Cuthbert's body was rested in the late 7th century in order to establish a church there — sadly nothing remains of this structure today. Another treasure is the cope of Henry II, left by that monarch in his will to Westminster Abbey, and later used by Henry VIII at the Field of the Cloth of Gold. Also housed are the embroidered cap of Sir Thomas Moore and Queen Catherine of Aragon's Chasuble and Dalmatics.

Stonyhurst and its gardens and grounds adjoining will remain a vivid memory for a lifetime and many visits will follow the first. The College has an open day once a year; details can be obtained from the College.

Stonyhurst to Shireburn Almshouses
Pass the front of the College and on approaching the observatory turn right through a gate. Follow the path to the end of Fox Fall Wood. Follow the path up and pass through the kissing-gate. Follow right-hand fence through a number of kissing-gates to the Almshouses.

Shireburn Almshouses, Hurst Green
'A rolling stone gathers no moss' the saying goes, but when the almshouses 'rolled' from Longridge Fell they gained a top storey. The almshouses were built in 1706, by Sir Nicolas Shireburn, and were originally sited on the east end of Longridge Fell. They consisted then of ten rooms and a chapel, with names over the doors of the villages from which the poor of Shireburn's lands were drawn: Aighton, Bailey, Chaigley, Dutton, Ribchester, Wiswell and Mitton.

In 1946 the almshouses were dismantled and rebuilt as workers' cottages at the College gates in Hurst Green. The plan is an adaption of the usual courtyard type employed in such institutions combined with an E-shaped house plan. The middle part of the main block was originally intended for the chapel, but has never been used as such. In reality the courtyard is a raised terrace approached by a stone balustrade with turned balusters. In the pediment (triangular low-pitched gable end of a 'Greek' temple-like building) are the arms of Shireburn with crest and supporters and below in large letters 'Shireburn Almshouses.'

Hurst Green to Merrick's Hall
Take the Longridge Road to the parish church of St. John the Evangelist, 1838. Here turn left onto the farm road down to Merrick's Hall.

Priest's House or Merrick's Hall
At the bottom of an old farm lane stands a dwelling that on first sight seems to be of little or no consequence. Closer inspection reveals a series of fine mullioned windows; the two to the right of the front

door have a transom as well. All this points to a house of the early 16th century. At that time it was a chantry priests' residence serving the chapel of St. John the Baptist at Bailey Hall. Within the house are some wood carvings on the oaken beams:

'ROBERTUS TAYLOR CANTORISTA HANC FABRICAM FECIT A. DNi M.D. XXIII'.

Robert Taylor was chaplain in 1517, and was still so in 1548 at 68 years of age.

Merrick's Hall to Bailey Hall
Pass through the farmyard into the field. Cross the field toward the tree-line to a point were a building is visible through the trees. Here find a gate to the right of a semi-circular corrugated iron hut. Through the gate, over the footbridge and on up to Bailey Hall.

Bailey Hall and Chapel of St. John the Baptist
Bailey Hall is the most intriguing and fascinating house in the district and warrants further investigation. Surrounded by a moat it is a T-shaped house with a profunity of mullioned windows, some with transom and mouldings. In days gone by the moat would be filled with cow dung and other delightful substances, which would indeed deter any unwanted oncomer with foul intent on the house's occupants. The Hall itself may be ascribed to the 16th century and probably marked the site of the original mansion of the Clitherow family that was built in the 1300s.

On the north side of the Hall are the fenced-off remains of the Chapel of St. John the Baptist. Only the crypt and exterior walling to a height of four feet remain. Founded by Robert de Clitherow about 1330, it is said to stand upon the site of an earlier chapel, but of this we only have a small mention in early 14th century documents. In 1549 the land was sold to William Eggleston and others, and no attempt was made to maintain service in the chapel. The building gradually fell into ruin, and the last remains were barbarously destroyed by order of its owner, Mr. Joseph Fenton, in 1830, notwithstanding an earnest remonstrance on the subject. It was a small chapel, without aisles, in a secluded situation. On the north side it was lighted by three pointed windows, exhibiting the curvilinear tracery of Edward II's time. At the west end was a bell gable. The tracery of the east window (which, as well as the windows of the south side, had been previously removed) is preserved among the much more recent architecture of the principal front of Stonyhurst College.

Tradition has it that the martyr Margaret Clitheroe, who was crushed to death beneath a board upon which heavy stones were placed, had her body taken from York to be buried in the family crypt at Bailey. Stydd Church also lays claim to the place of burial — an unusually shallow coffin in the crypt is said to be her last resting place. Oddly enough I have seen what is claimed to be her head. This last relic is contained in a box in the vaults of Mitton Church. Crushed to death, then cut-up for relics — poor woman to suffer such a fate.

Bailey Hall to Dutton Hall

Follow farm lane up, over cattle-grid, past the hen-house standing in the field on the right, to a lone tree on the right of the road. Walk on for 80 paces then bear left of the road and walk directly forward to what seems to be a stile in the far fence. At the 'stile' cross the footbridge then walk across the field on a slight left-diagonal to go over a stile on the edge of the wood (the stile is in a shallow valley by a lone tree on the edge of the wood). Down and over the footbridge and up to the farm road via a stile. Walk up the road to Grindlestone House. Pass through the farmyard and over the stile. Follow right-hand fence on, over the next two stiles, then follow left-hand fence, crossing three stiles to the roadway. Walk down to Dutton Hall.

Dutton Hall

Standing high above Ribchester Bridge is the fine old residence of Dutton Hall, with claim to a magnificent view of Salesbury and Wilpshire. The manor of Dutton was given, in 1102, to Robert de Lacy by Henry I, and from that time it became a member of the honour of Clitheroe. In 1290 the manor passed to Henry de Clayton of Clayton-le-Dale, and descended regularly till 1400. The next principle family was the Towneleys, appearing about 1380. The present house was built by Richard Towneley around 1670 in the time of Charles II.

The house has a hall with two cross wings with a splendid bay to the hall centre. The bay is square and over-mighty. It has seven-light transomed openings on both ground and first floor. The top of the bay has a balustrade with turned balusters, a good resting spot on a fine summer's day. A few years ago the house was in use as an orphanage — a finer setting for such an institution would be hard to find and many a fine adventure must have been had by its occupants.

The illustration below shows Lower Dutton Cottages on Gallows Lane, leading to Dutton Hall; the lane is so called after the gibbet that stood further up the road at Three Turns. A local highwayman, known as Tom King, was displayed on the gibbet having been tried and hung for his crimes. Before his capture the unfortunate rogue is said to have sought refuge in the Fenton Arms (now the Punch Bowl Inn, dated 1793).

Dutton Hall to Stonebridge

Walk to the front of the Hall and pass through the wooden gate on your left. Turn right and walk towards the large round blue tank. Keeping the tank on your left, walk on, over a large pipe to the left of a field wall. Follow the wall down to go over a stile. Walk down to the brook and walk downstream to a footbridge. Cross and walk up to go over a field stile. Follow left-hand fence to a gate and double stile. Over stiles and walk straight down the hill, between two old ponds, to go over a stile by a gate. Follow the sheep track down to go over a footbridge. Turn right and head for the left-hand corner of the field, keeping the farm on your left, to go over a stile. Follow left-hand fence, over the footbridge, over the stile, then follow left-hand fence down to Stonebridge.

*   *   *

I think you will now agree that this has been a most enjoyable and rewarding walk, one you will return to many times, and hopefully each time see a little more of what it has to offer. If you are not too eager to return home then may I suggest that you visit the village of Ribchester? A Roman Museum contains many fine artifacts and a Roman granary and bath-house have been excavated and renovated, all being part of the Roman fort of Bremetennacum. The Museum is open daily: February–May 14.00–17.00; June–August 11.30–17.30; September–November 14.00–17.00; December–January Saturday only 14.00–17.00. Small admission charge. Tel. Ribchester (025484) 261.